I'm Still Rising

A Book of Poems

Inspired by a Black Woman's Journey of

Rising

From Nights of Terror and Fear
To a Daybreak that's Wondrously Clear

Omeshia Bowens

Cover design by Dr. A. Giselle Jones-Jones of The Write Source TWCS & Publishing, LLC

Published by The Write Source TWCS & Publishing, LLC | Jamestown, NC

PRINTED IN THE UNITED STATES OF AMERICA
Library of Congress Cataloguing-in-Publication Data
A catalog record for this book is available from the Library of Congress.

ISBN 978-1-7355578-3-0

$9.95 U.S.

This book is dedicated to my daughters and every young girl / woman who is still rising.

Contents

Acknowledgements

Writing a book is harder than I thought yet more rewarding than I could have ever imagined. Writing poetry is a part of my healing journey. I use writing as a form of therapy.

I would like to thank God, my deceased Grandmother Essie, who raised me and taught me to pray at a very early age, and my mother Lynn – for without her, there would be no me.

To my deceased Aunt Betti Jo Godwin, who first introduced me to poetry and helped me write my first poem at age six, I dedicate this book of poems to your precious spirit.

To my three beautiful daughters, who encourage, inspire, and motivate me to keep fighting to be successful, my hope is that I will set a positive example and be someone you can be proud of. I would also like to thank my spiritual Godmother Hannah who took me under her wing and taught me the importance of prayer and giving thanks to God and my ancestors. She also helped me learn the importance of self-love.

Finally, I would like to thank my Publishing company The Write Source TWCS & Publishing and my editor, Dr. A Giselle Jones-Jones, for helping to make my dream of publishing a book come true.

Fatherless Father's Day

No one to give ties, socks & a card to
No one to celebrate and hug tight
No one to teach a son how to be a man
or show a daughter how a man should
love her right.

No one to call a hero or someone to
protect you who is big & strong.
No one to tell I love you & lecture you
when you're wrong

Mothers are irreplaceable
But they could never take a father's
place
So, I say a little prayer for the
fatherless child.
On each and every Father's Day!

A Daughter's Prayer

God, please heal my mother in all the
places she is hurt.
Help her be at peace & discover her
self-worth.

Soften her heart & help her see,
it's ok to be proud of your daughter,
instead of jealous of me.

I plead to you, O Lord, help her to
understand
The validation she seeks will never
come from a man!

Heal me, too, God! Help me to let go of
the pain.
Growing up with a toxic mother who
feels for me such disdain.

Break the generational curse of toxic
mother-daughter relationships.

Heal the trauma of my absent father that reflects in the choices of every type of man that we pick.

Old Soul

You've got an old soul, girl – is what
the old folks used to say to me.
You'd rather listen to Betty Wright
than to the latest R&B.

You've got an old soul, girl –
You've got that look in your eyes
that tells many stories of rebirth
from all your past lives.

You've got an old soul, girl –
wise beyond your years, it's true.
You must listen to your spirit of
discernment and let it guide you.

You've got an old soul, girl –
Yes, you have been here many times
before
feeding your soul's desire to learn
lessons to overcome more and more.

A Black Woman's Strength

A Black Woman's strength comes from
being born into a world where she feels
undervalued, unloved, and unprotected
day after day.
Her only option is to be strong when
the world has knocked her flat on her
face.

She is often the scapegoat for the
problems of the world;
It's hard being born as a little black
girl.

Famous poet Zora Neal Hurston
referred to black women as *mules*:
the lowest on the totem pole in a world
so cruel.

Dehumanized, oversexualized,
tormented throughout history –
As a Black woman, I feel I am only
strong because there is no other option
for me.

Ancestor Angels

Our Ancestors are our Angels,
their energy never dies
Their essences are still with us
throughout our day to day lives.

Meditate and listen with your heart,
and you will soon discover,
You are surrounded by many ancestors
— from both your father and mother.

Watching over you, protecting you,
guiding you, and keeping you safe,
In their celestial arms,
there's no safer place.

I Will, I Am, I Can

I will forgive…. myself for all my past mistakes and self-sabotaging behavior. I was operating in survival mode; I was blind but now I see.

I am loved… I am worthy… No one is perfect - especially not the ones who have talked down to, lied on, and criticized me.

I can … learn from mistakes and all that I have been through, for it was a part of my path on my journey to succeed.

I will… I am… I can…. as long as I believe.

Unborn Child

To my unborn child that I never got a chance to know,

I often daydream of what you would have been like if I had kept you and watched you grow. Unborn Child, please forgive me. I question my decision every day. I pray that you are up in heaven, and I will get to meet you some day.

Unborn child, at the time I felt I was doing what was best for me and you. Protecting you from the pain of a world so cruel. I prayed for forgiveness from God, myself, and you,

The unborn child I never knew.

Emotionless Black Man

Black Man, it's ok to cry.
It doesn't make you weak;
don't keep your feelings inside.

Black Man, you are worthy and loved
in every way.
It seems like the world has a target on
your back –
you must always watch what you do
and say.

You were taught from an early age that
real men don't cry,
so, you have suffered in silence
full of hurt and don't understand why.

It's because you are hurting from all
the emotions that you keep bottled
inside.

Black man, let it out.
It's ok to cry.

Purpose

Pain has purpose and
      purpose endures pain ~~
like the moon needs the sky and
plants need rain.

We have to go through it
      to grow through it ~~
for it helps shape, build, and mold us
into who we are meant to be.

The good and the bad
      were all a part of the plan ~~
like the waves of the ocean and sea.

Continue to sail on ~~
like the current as the ocean flows.

Pain has purpose ~~

It was meant to nourish your soul.

The Strongest People

I laugh so hard to keep from crying,
Fighting back tears because inside I'm
dying.

Everywhere I go I wear a smile.
Often the life of the party,
center of the crowd.

Smiling, laughing, and telling jokes,
all the while hurting inside,
feeling sad and broke.

No one knows these secrets I keep
inside.
I just smile day to day and my sadness
I hide.

Surrounded by lots of people,
yet I feel so alone.
They all look to me for advice and
admiration, so I pretend to be strong.

Soul Tie

You sex me and suck me,
but do you really love me?
You give me intimacy
satisfying me physically,
but what about nurturing my
intellectual side and my soul
spiritually?

You make me climax back to back
but can't stimulate my mind.
I need more than just sex.
You treat me like an object and have
no respect.

I deserve love and affection along with
intimacy, too.
The more we have sex,
the more my body yearns for you.

I know it's not love but can't seem to
cut you off, and I don't understand
why.
Ladies, be careful who you are sexing –
because I'm bound by a soul tie.

Generational Curses

Generational Curses, you must set free
a whole new mindset as I rise from
poverty.

Generational Curses, you will no longer
hold me back. That train is derailed on
a new track.

New Blessings, New Mindset, New
Money coming to me. I will bear new
fruit on my family tree.

Using strength & knowledge from my
ancestors, I will have victory.

Breaking Generational Curses –
I am the key!!

Breaking Chains

Let's Normalize falling in love with someone that you don't have to give a second or third chance because they came correct & got it right the 1st time around!

Let's Normalize not being told to stick with your marriage even though it's physically, mentally & emotionally beating you down!

Let's Normalize the power of self-love and start protecting and uplifting our black men & women.

Try sticking together instead of being in competition. No more Light Skin versus dark skin because we are all one in the same.

Let's break the generational curses of the Willie Lynch chains.

Compare

Never compete or try to compare
because you will just end up in secret
competition
with a person who's not even aware.

Steady worrying about someone else's
life instead of your own.
Broke pockets
watching counting someone else's coins.

What the next person is eating won't
digest your food!

Focus on your own table and what's
good for you.

Empty Cup

I used to always pour into other people's cups until one day I had nothing left to pour.

I gladly filled up other people like they were cars & I was a gas pump at the convenience store.

Pouring way too much into others . . . my own cup went dry.

Now my calls go unanswered and texts with no reply.

I was left drained of my finances & all my beautiful energy, too.

I now realize my cup went empty from over pouring & being misused.

I don't pity myself or look for sympathy-

It just taught me to never pour into someone else while my own cup goes empty.

Growing up Poor

Growing up as a young girl I didn't
know that I was poor until society told
me.
How could I be poor if Grandma made
sure we never went hungry?

I thought poor people didn't have
clothes or shoes to wear.
Grandma made sure my feet were never
bare.

I kept a new dress because my
Grandma used fabric to sew.
She kept my hair neatly braided with
beads and bows.

Yes, I didn't know I was poor until
society told me.
We received government assistance and
lived in poverty.

Looking back, it was probably the only
time in my life that I felt safe and
everything seemed right.

Poverty to me is more than lack of
physical needs but is also a state of
mind.
I felt rich with love and wish I could go
back in time.

"I Am" Poem

I am a single black mother with three
daughters
I wonder if black people will ever
receive reparations
I hear an echo of my grandmother's
voice
I see visions of me going places
I want to be successful and wealthy
I am a single black mother with three
daughters

I pretend to be strong
I feel like I am living a lie
I touch the heavens with my prayer as
they rise high in the sky
I worry about not being successful
I cry when I feel overwhelmed
I am a single black mother with three
daughters

I understand everything happens for a reason
I say God makes no mistakes.
I dream of being successful with a big house on the lake
I try to put my all into achieving my goals.
I hope to be successful
I am a single black mother with three daughters

Today, I choose Me

Today, I decided to choose me.

I decided I will no longer hang on to dead situations out of fear of what I cannot see.

I will no longer try to control others.

I will focus on accountability for myself.
I will no longer be afraid to reach out if I need help.

I am beautiful and deserving of someone pouring back into me.

Everything I have poured into to others . . .

It is my time to receive.

Confidence

Tore down my self-confidence before I even knew what self-confidence was . . .

Made me feel ugly when I should have felt loved . . .

Called me names & made jokes about my skinny little body & big bucked teeth.

Childhood trauma cuts so deep!

I'm damn near 40 & still insecure about my smile . . .

Guess I'm still healing from when my family joked that I was ugly as a child.

A Reflection That Speaks

I look at my reflection on the sunset of
the lake silently gazing back at me.
Reflecting in the mirror of myself
the inner me that no one knows —
the deepest part of my ripened soul.

The part of me that knows my purpose.
The part of me that is not afraid to let
go. The part of me that thinks that I'm
beautiful from head to toe.
The part of me that is healed.

All the shadow work has been done.
All the fights have been fought and all
battles are victorious and have been
won.

As I gaze in the water in the reflection,
I see a beautiful divine soul staring back
at me.

Why, Lord?

Why was I given such tough life lessons
to learn in this game of life?

Why was I the one chosen to be made
strong & to go through such strife?

Why must I struggle to be successful &
endure such pain & harm?

I know that you promised "trouble
don't last always" –
but I'm tired of weathering the storm.

I pray really hard!
Lord, I promise I'm trying to keep my
faith, but I can't seem to shake my
feelings of wanting to escape.

Why couldn't I have had a rich mom &
dad to nurture me & love me right,

To tuck me in & read me bedtime
stories at night?
Why have you allowed me to be hurt
over & over, Lord, and to be misused &
abused,

When others seem to get things easy in
life? Lord, I'm tired & overworked &
confused.

Why, why, why, Lord?

I'm just trying to understand.
I'm praying really hard and doing all I
can.

Mirrors

I like mirrors because mirrors like me.
It took me a long time to learn to love
myself unapologetically.

Some say that mirrors are windows to
the soul,
So, as I gaze at my reflection and speak
my life goals.

I shout positive affirmations into the
mirror, and the affirmations reflect
back at me.

I love mirrors because they help me
succeed.

Ancestors Got My Back

My Ancestors don't play about me.
They watch over me day to day.

Watching, guiding and protecting
Making sure I'm safe.

I warn you with caution:
Do me wrong if you dare.

My ancestors fight my battles.
My army stays prepared.

There is a lot of power in my bloodline.
So, it's best if you just leave me be.

One thing I know for sure is my
ancestors don't play about me.

Domestically Silenced

Domestically Silenced from Domestic
Violence

Black eyes, battered, broken,
hurt and confused,
lip busted –
my body was bruised.

He screamed as he beat me,
"The police can't help you!"
I called 911 but to my dismay,
the police didn't care;
they took us both in that day.

My eyes were opened.
I began to understand why . . .
Victims of Domestic Violence
don't call the police
when being beaten by a man.

Protection Against Envy and Jealousy Prayer

God, protect me from the spirit of jealousy, create within me a heart that rejoices when I see others who are blessed...

Bind up the spirit of Jealousy within or against me so that I can be ready to receive my blessings next...

Grant me with divine perception to see all that I already have to be thankful for...

Guide my footsteps as I prosper in order to keep me humble as you continue to bless me with more...

Elevate my status and use me to be a blessing to others, Lord, in everything that I do...

Strengthen my spirit of discernment so I can never be misused.

Asé Amen 🙏 ▨